ECOFACTS

CLIMATE CHANGE

ECO FACTS

IZZI HOWELL

CRABTREE
PUBLISHING COMPANY
WWW.CRABTREEBOOKS.COM

CRABTREE
PUBLISHING COMPANY
WWW.CRABTREEBOOKS.COM

Author: Izzi Howell

Editorial director: Kathy Middleton

Editors: Izzi Howell, Ellen Rodger

Proofreader: Melissa Boyce

Designer: Clare Nicholas

Cover designer: Steve Mead

Prepress technician: Tammy McGarr

Print coordinator: Katherine Berti

Photo credits:
Getty: helt2 6, Per-Anders Pettersson 15b, FRISO GENTSCH/AF 17, sal73it 19b, Robert_Ford 21t, Photographer, Videographer, Writer 25l, Lemanieh 25r, Karl Spencer 26t; National Snow and Ice Data Center: Nick Cobbing/Greenpeace 13t; Shutterstock: Designua 9, FloridaStock 11t, Sk Hasan Ali 11b, Red monkey 12, gary yim 13b, Earl D. Walker 15t, Artisticco 18, Amanda Nicholls 19t, Tomacco 20, hikrcn 21b, testing 23, ProStockStudio 24, GraphicsRF 26, AMFPhotography 26b.

All design elements from Shutterstock.

Every attempt has been made to clear copyright. Should there be any inadvertent omission please apply to the publisher for rectification.

The website addresses (URLs) included in this book were valid at the time of going to press. However, it is possible that contents or addresses may have changed since the publication of this book. No responsibility for any such changes can be accepted by either the author or the Publisher.

Library and Archives Canada Cataloguing in Publication

Title: Climate change eco facts / Izzi Howell.
Names: Howell, Izzi, author.
Description: Series statement: Eco facts | Includes index.
Identifiers: Canadiana (print) 20190087951 |
  Canadiana (ebook) 2019008796X |
  ISBN 9780778763451 (hardcover) |
  ISBN 9780778763574 (softcover) |
  ISBN 9781427123435 (HTML)Subjects: LCSH: Climatic changes—
Juvenile literature. | LCSH: Global warming—Juvenile literature. |
LCSH: Nature—Effect of human beings on—Juvenile literature.
Classification: LCC QC903.15 .H69 2019 | DDC j363.738/74—dc23

Library of Congress Cataloging-in-Publication Data

Names: Howell, Izzi, author.
Title: Climate change eco facts / Izzi Howell.
Description: New York, New York : Crabtree Publishing, 2020. |
Series: Eco facts | Includes bibliographical references and index.
Identifiers: LCCN 2019014530 (print) | LCCN 2019020548 (ebook) |
  ISBN 9781427123435 (Electronic) |
  ISBN 9780778763451 (hardcover : alk. paper) |
  ISBN 9780778763574 (pbk. : alk. paper)
Subjects: LCSH: Climatic changes--Juvenile literature. |
  Global environmental change--Juvenile literature.
Classification: LCC QC903.15 (ebook) | LCC QC903.15 .H68 2020 (print)
  | DDC 363.738/74--dc23
LC record available at https://lccn.loc.gov/2019014530

Crabtree Publishing Company
www.crabtreebooks.com   1–800–387–7650
Published by Crabtree Publishing Company in 2020
©2019 The Watts Publishing Group.

Printed in the U.S.A./072019/CG20190501

Published in Canada
Crabtree Publishing
616 Welland Ave.
St. Catharines, Ontario
L2M 5V6

Published in the United States
Crabtree Publishing
PMB 59051
350 Fifth Avenue, 59th Floor
New York, New York 10118

Contents

What is climate change?

Temperature changes are normal on Earth. Throughout our planet's history, there have been periods of cooler and warmer temperatures, which have happened naturally. However, Earth is now warmer than at any point over the last 650,000 years. Most scientists agree that today's climate change has been made more extreme by human activity.

Causes

methane gas released by livestock (page 14)

some fertilizers (page 8)

deforestation (page 14)

burning fossil fuels (page 6)

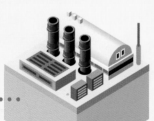

burning biomass (wood, plants)

97% of climate scientists agree that the current changes in climate are due to human activity.

By 2050, **200 million** people may have had to leave their homes because of climate change.

Threats

Climate change is a huge threat to life on Earth. Its effect on the natural environment could result in the destruction of many habitats and the extinction of some plants and animals. It is also affecting the places where humans live, as well as our food supply.

desertification (page 20)

rising temperatures (page 9)

melting polar ice (page 10)

wildfires

flooding (page 11)

extreme weather (page 24)

habitat loss

animal extinction

Stopping climate change

Since humans play a large role in contributing to climate change, we have a responsibility to stop it from happening. Most of the activity that causes climate change comes from industry. However, we can all make changes to help slow down climate change, from planting trees to using **renewable** electricity sources.

Fossil fuels

Oil, natural gas, and coal are all examples of fossil fuels. **They are burned to power factories and vehicles, and to create electricity. The use of fossil fuels is a major cause of climate change.**

Sources

Fossil fuels come from underground. They formed over millions of years, from the remains of dead plants and animals. Oil and natural gas are pumped out of the ground through deep, narrow holes. Coal is mined below ground and at Earth's surface.

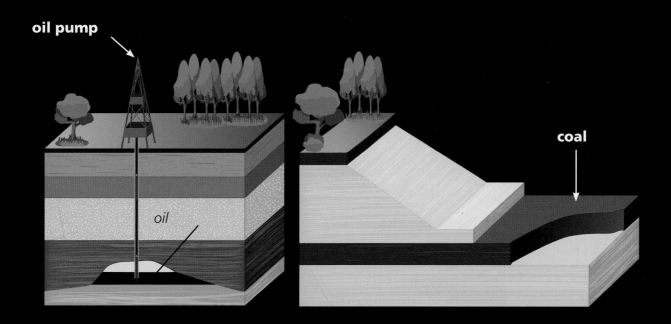

oil pump

oil

coal

Burning fossil fuels

When fossil fuels are burned, they give off heat energy. This heat energy is used to create power. However, burning fossil fuels also gives off carbon dioxide (CO_2). Carbon dioxide is a **greenhouse gas** (see page 8), which contributes to climate change.

Burning coal is the single largest cause of climate change.

A coal-fired power plant releases carbon dioxide into the atmosphere.

Going, going, gone

Since the beginning of the **Industrial Revolution** in the 1700s, we have used huge amounts of fossil fuels. The amount of oil, natural gas, and coal left on Earth is running low. We are using more fossil fuels than ever before because our population is increasing. If we continue to use fossil fuels at the same rate or faster, we may run out in the next 100 years.

Making a change

Many people are starting to choose alternative energy sources now (see panel below), before fossil fuels run out forever. Leaving fossil fuels in the ground and changing over to different energy sources will help to slow down the rate of climate change.

Fossil fuel dependent

Some less economically developed countries depend on fossil fuels for their economy. They can't afford to switch to alternative energy sources. Without fossil fuels, they couldn't produce enough income to support their citizens and further develop their country. However, these less economically developed countries also tend to be near the equator, and are among those most affected by climate change.

One small step

Could your school install solar panels? In some countries, groups raise funds to buy and install solar panels at schools and community centers. After they are in place, the panels use fewer fossil fuels and save money on energy bills.

Alternative energy

We can use power from the Sun, the wind, and moving water to create electricity. As these natural power sources will never run out, we don't need to worry about our supply ending, as we do with fossil fuels. They also don't create any greenhouse gases, so they have no negative impact on climate change.

Global warming

Global warming is a part of climate change. The average temperature on Earth is increasing because of the greenhouse effect. This is a natural process that traps heat from the Sun close to Earth.

Greenhouse gases

The greenhouse effect is caused by certain gases, which are known as greenhouse gases. Greenhouse gases are produced both naturally and by human activity.

Greenhouse gas	Produced in nature by	Produced by humans through
Carbon dioxide	Breathing / Volcanic eruptions	Burning fossil fuels / Vehicles
Water vapor	Evaporation from rivers and seas	Burning fossil fuels
Methane	**Decomposing** plants	Animal farming
Nitrous oxide	Bacteria in soil	Soil fertilizers

The atmosphere

Earth is surrounded by an atmosphere—a layer of gases that stretches from directly above the ground to about 6,200 miles (10,000 km) into space. The atmosphere blocks harmful radiation from the Sun, but lets in light and heat. After greenhouse gases are produced, they collect in the atmosphere above Earth's surface.

Trapped heat

During the day, light and heat from the Sun pass through the atmosphere and warm Earth's surface. At night, heat from the surface should travel back out into the air as Earth cools down. However, some of the heat is trapped close to Earth by greenhouse gases in the atmosphere. This makes the temperature on the surface increase.

Global warming doesn't just result in hotter weather. It can also cause more rain and snow in some areas (see pages 24–25).

Warm but not too hot

0°F
(–18°C)

The greenhouse effect is necessary for life on Earth. Without it, the average temperature on Earth would be around 0°Fahrenheit (–18°C). This is too cold for many plants and animals to survive year round. The large amounts of greenhouse gases created by human activity are making the greenhouse effect much more extreme.

A global impact

The natural environment is very sensitive. Even a small increase in temperature can have big consequences. Global warming caused by the greenhouse effect is impacting many different parts of the world, including the polar ice caps (see pages 10–13), coasts (see page 11), and coral reefs (see page 17).

Some heat from the Sun bounces straight off the surface of Earth and back out into space.

atmosphere

greenhouse gases

Rising sea levels

Climate change has a significant impact on the oceans and seas. The increase in temperature is causing sea levels to rise and destroy ocean habitats.

The oceans have absorbed **90%** of the extra heat caused by the greenhouse effect.

Warm water

The rise in temperature on Earth is heating up the oceans. When water warms up, it expands and takes up more space than cool water. This is causing sea levels to rise around the world. Half of the rise in sea levels in the past century is because of warm water expansion.

Ice sheets

Huge blocks of ice cover the land and the oceans at Earth's north and south poles. These ice sheets are made up of a huge amount of frozen freshwater. There are also blocks of sea ice, which are formed of frozen saltwater.

Melting ice

Warmer air temperatures are causing the ice sheets to melt. When the ice sheets melt, the water from the ice travels into the ocean. This additional water makes the sea levels rise.

Scientists estimate that the sea levels will have risen by 11 to 39 inches (28 to 98 cm) by 2100. If all the polar ice melted, sea levels would rise by up to 23 feet (7 m).

Habitat destruction

As the ice sheets melt, the habitats of many polar animals that live and hunt on the ice, such as polar bears, are being destroyed. Polar bears hunt seals from holes in the sea ice where seals come up to breathe. With less sea ice, polar bears have fewer opportunities to catch seals to eat. Many are starving to death.

A polar bear waits on the ice for a seal to appear.

Dangers

Rising sea levels are causing flooding in low coastal areas. This threatens the homes and businesses of millions of people. By 2100, the homes of 275 million people around the world could be flooded. Most of the people vulnerable to flooding live in South and Southeast Asia.

Not enough salt

Melting ice sheets also affect underwater **ecosystems**, because the water from the ice sheets is freshwater. This **dilutes** the saltwater of the ocean. Ocean wildlife, such as sharks, need saltwater to survive, so they will be harmed if the water becomes less salty.

Flooding is already common in Bangladesh—one of the countries most vulnerable to rising sea levels. By 2050, as many as 25 million people in Bangladesh could be affected.

The Greenland ice sheet

The surface of Greenland is covered in the second-largest ice sheet on Earth. It is made up of layers of snow packed tightly together. The Greenland ice sheet has already started melting. If it melts entirely, it will have serious consequences around the world.

FACT FILE

LOCATION:
Greenland

SIZE:
660,000 square miles (1,710,000 sq km)

THICKNESS:
1.9 miles (3 km)

Greenland

Icebergs

As the ice sheet melts, large chunks can break away from it. These chunks move into the ocean as icebergs. The icebergs can block the path of ships and cause great damage if the ships collide with them.

Ice cycle

Every year, the Greenland ice sheet gains ice in the winter from fallen snow. In summer, some ice melts away. However, its average mass shouldn't change too much as it regains in winter what it loses in summer. This is no longer the case, due to climate change. The ice sheet is now losing much more ice than it gains.

The melting Greenland ice sheet alone is adding 0.04 inches (1 mm) per year to rising sea levels.

Causes

Experts aren't sure why the Greenland ice sheet is melting so quickly. It sits on land, so it should melt more slowly than sea ice, which melts quickly when it comes into contact with warm water. Scientists think it may be part of a natural cycle of ice loss and gain, made worse by climate change.

Scientists are drilling down into the deep ice that formed hundreds of years ago, hoping this research will help them understand why the ice is melting so quickly.

Dark ice

One reason for the excess melting could be the color of the ice. When the top layer of ice melts away, it exposes older, darker ice beneath the surface. This ice's dark color means that it absorbs more light from the Sun and melts more quickly.

Colored algae can also grow on the surface of the ice, making it darker and quicker to melt.

Weather threats

If the Greenland ice sheet completely melted, the height of the island would be much lower. This would affect air circulation around the Arctic. At the moment, storms "bounce" off Greenland and back into the ocean. If this didn't happen, the storms would carry on toward other countries in the North Atlantic Ocean.

Protecting the ice

One possible way to preserve the ice could be to wrap it in white blankets. The white color of the blankets would reflect sunlight away, reducing the amount of ice melted.

Farming and food

Farming and food supply are closely connected to climate change. The production of some types of food, such as beef, contribute to climate change, while some crops have been negatively affected by global warming.

Raising livestock is responsible for producing 14.5 percent of all greenhouse gases.

Animal farming

Raising animals such as cattle, sheep, and chickens for their meat, milk, leather, wool, and eggs contributes to greenhouse gases. Growing food to feed the animals increases the use of fossil fuels, takes up more land, and contributes to water and air pollution. Grazing animals also release methane, a greenhouse gas. Different parts of the world produce different amounts of methane depending on the methods of animal farming used.

Deforestation

Large areas of forest and grassland have been cleared to make room for **livestock** farms. **Deforestation** contributes to climate change, as fewer plants and trees exist to absorb carbon dioxide from the atmosphere, increasing the greenhouse effect. Plants absorb carbon dioxide as part of **photosynthesis**, which gives the plants energy to survive.

Crops

Plants are easily affected by changes in weather caused by climate change. They can be scorched if temperatures are too high, drowned by too much rain, or dry out in periods of **drought**. This can cause entire crops to fail, leaving farmers with no income and whole communities with no food supply.

These stalks of corn have not developed properly due to drought and very high temperatures.

The future of food

Food supply will certainly be affected by future climate change. Many countries will struggle to grow enough food to support their population. This will hit less economically developed countries particularly hard, as they can't afford to import food. However, some northern areas, such as Canada, predict that they will be able to grow more crops as temperatures rise.

Farmers in Malawi struggle to grow crops after years of drought.

One small step

Buy local and seasonal food when possible. Avoid foods that have traveled a long way.

Food transportation

In the past, people could only eat food that grew in their local area at certain times of year. This has changed thanks to quick food transportation, which allows us to eat food from around the world all year round. However, the planes, trucks, and ships carrying food burn fuel and release greenhouse gases, contributing to climate change.

Habitats and wildlife

Climate change is having a huge impact on the natural world. Many plants and animals are losing their habitats and food supplies, putting them at risk of extinction. Others are finding new places to live.

Food chains

Every living thing in an ecosystem is connected through food chains. If just one plant or animal becomes less common or dies out as a result of climate change, it affects every other living thing as well. They may have less food to eat or there may be more predators that eat them. This results in a chain reaction across the entire ecosystem.

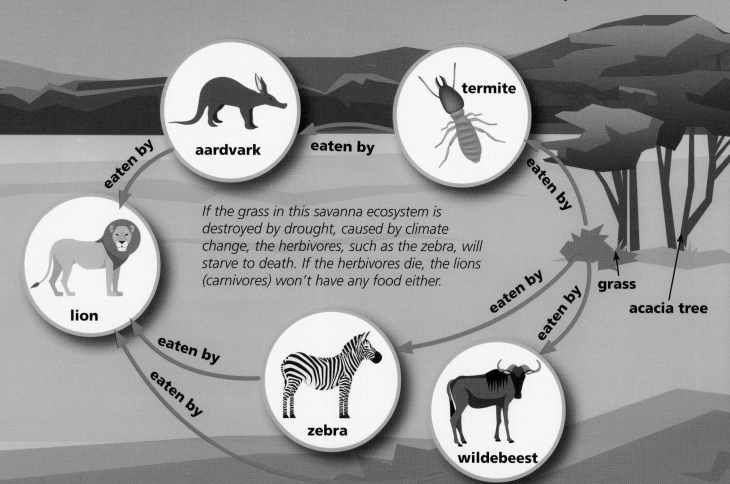

If the grass in this savanna ecosystem is destroyed by drought, caused by climate change, the herbivores, such as the zebra, will starve to death. If the herbivores die, the lions (carnivores) won't have any food either.

aardvark   eaten by   termite

eaten by

grass

acacia tree

eaten by   eaten by

lion

eaten by

zebra   eaten by   wildebeest

eaten by

Plant life cycles

Climate change can affect plants' life cycles. Plants are starting to flower earlier in the year as the temperature is warmer. This means that some flowers may not get **pollinated**, as the insects that pollinate them are not around at the right time. Plants also produce fruit earlier, which may make it hard for animals to survive in autumn, as the fruit that they depend on for food appeared too early.

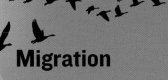

Migration

Some animals, such as birds and fish, migrate. They move to different areas at different times of the year, looking for food, warmer temperatures, or a mate. Migration is triggered by the seasons, so changes in temperature caused by climate change can confuse animals' migration patterns.

On the move

As a result of climate change, other animals are moving into new areas where it was once too cold for them to survive. This is affecting the food chains in these habitats, as the ecosystem adjusts to include new animals that need to find food. New species are being produced as plants and animals reproduce with species that move into their habitat.

The pizzly bear is a mix between a polar bear and a grizzly bear. These species have interbred for the first time because of global warming. Some polar bears have moved south into grizzly bear territory to look for food, as their ice habitat melts.

An acidic ocean

Oceans absorb about 30 percent of the carbon dioxide in the atmosphere. As the amount of CO_2 in the atmosphere increases, so does the level of CO_2 in the oceans. This is making oceans more acidic. This acidity damages the shells of ocean animals, such as clams and oysters.

Coral is unable to grow in acidic water and eventually dissolves.

coral

clams

Sea turtles

Sea turtles are particularly vulnerable to climate change, as they depend on both ocean and beach habitats at different points of their life. If global warming continues, these animals, and the ecosystems in which they live, could be at serious risk.

FACT FILE

LOCATION:
All oceans, except the polar regions

NUMBER OF SPECIES: **7**

THREATS:
Climate change, habitat loss, poaching

Sea and beach

Adult sea turtles spend most of their lives at sea. They come on land to lay their eggs on beaches every few years. Having access to safe beaches where their eggs can be laid and hatched is key to the survival of sea turtles.

Beach destruction

Rising sea levels are already destroying the beaches where sea turtles lay their eggs, leaving the sea turtles with nowhere to go. Sea turtle eggs are also washed away by waves, which are coming higher up the beach than ever before.

Coral reefs

Hawksbill sea turtles often live in coral reefs. They feed on sea sponges that grow among the coral. The destruction of coral reefs, caused by the acidification of the oceans (see page 17), is threatening these turtles that depend on coral reefs for food.

The hawksbill sea turtle uses its sharp beak to grab bites of sea sponge.

99% of sea turtles born on one Australian island are female. In the 1970s, only **83%** were born female.

Hot sand

If sea turtle eggs are laid in hot sand, the turtle that hatches is likely to be female. Rising temperatures are causing a very high number of certain sea turtles to be born female. In the short term, this can help sea turtle numbers, as there are more females who can lay eggs. However, if too few male turtles are born, not enough sea turtles will be able to reproduce.

Protecting turtles

As well as working to reduce climate change, people are protecting sea turtles in more direct ways. Sea turtle nesting beaches are being built up to stop them being eroded by rising sea levels. **Conservationists** are moving turtle nests to shady or protected areas where the temperature of the sand can be controlled.

These sea turtle eggs have been reburied in a safe place.

Desertification

Desertification is when fertile land is destroyed and becomes dry land where nothing can grow. This process happens as a result of climate change and human activity.

Plants are killed off by high temperatures caused by climate change.

Humans cut down trees for their wood or clear land for livestock farming.

Soil can lose its nutrients if farmers don't fertilize it, so plants can't grow in it any longer.

LOSS OF PLANTS

Soil erosion

Plant roots help to hold soil together. Once plants and their roots are gone, soil is much more vulnerable to **erosion**. The top layers of soil are easily blown away by wind or washed away by water. This exposes lower, less fertile layers of soil where no plants can grow.

One small step

It's important to give nutrients back to the soil. Keep a compost bin of fruit and vegetable waste at home or at school and fertilize the soil with the compost you make. Find a link on page 31.

Grassland grazing

For many years, people thought that **grazing** livestock contributed to desertification in grassland areas. They believed that the animals ate too many plants, leading to soil erosion. So, they removed the livestock, but the desertification continued. Later, people realized that the grassland ecosystem depends on grazing animals. The animals fertilize the soil with their waste and help to mix up the soil when they are migrating or running away from predators. However, too much livestock can overgraze grasslands and contribute to climate change in other ways (see page 14).

Solving the problem

Desertified lands are home to about one-sixth of the world's population. However, nearly all of these people live in less economically developed countries. It can be hard for the governments of these countries to find the resources to address the issue of desertification.

Causing climate change

Desertification isn't just a consequence of climate change. It's also a cause of climate change. Plants take in carbon dioxide. When plants are lost in the process of desertification, there are fewer plants available to absorb carbon dioxide. This increases the amount of carbon dioxide in the atmosphere.

A desertified area in Burkina Faso, Africa.

Fear and fighting

Desertification can lead to **conflict**. When land becomes a desert, crops can no longer be grown and water sources dry up. Shortages of food and water in desertified areas can lead to fighting, as people argue over resources. Desertification can also force people to leave their homes and become **refugees**.

Many people in Somalia have fled to refugee camps in Kenya, escaping violence from a civil war, as well as food shortages caused by desertification and drought.

21

FOCUS ON

Desertification in China

Desertification is a serious problem in northern China. Deserts are quickly approaching major cities, threatening homes and affecting the country's food supply.

FACT FILE

 LOCATION:
Asia

 AMOUNT OF LAND THAT IS DESERTIFIED:
27.4 percent

 NUMBER AFFECTED:
400 million people

History

Desertification has been an issue in China since the 1950s, when forests and fields were destroyed to build new cities. Workers built on the cleared land and used the wood for construction. The undeveloped cleared land became desert.

The Gobi Desert in China absorbs **1,390** square miles (3,600 sq km) of grassland every year. It is the fastest-growing desert on Earth.

Removing the trees has made it easier for the wind to carry sand to new areas and for existing deserts to expand.

1

2

Sandstorms

Sandstorms are becoming more common in northern China as a result of desertification. In some areas, they happen three to 10 times a month. Sandstorms damage crops and cause pollution. In China's already polluted cities, they make air quality and visibility even worse.

The sand and pollution in the air over Beijing, China, makes visibility very poor.

Food shortages

The loss of farmland results in a decrease in food supply, as farmers have nowhere to grow crops. China's population is also increasing, which puts even more pressure on the food supply. China may experience food shortages if desertification continues at its current rate.

People

An increasing number of people in China are environmental refugees, forced to leave their homes because of desertification. Some of these refugees are farmers who have lost their farmland. With no way to earn a living, they are forced to move away in search of work.

Finding solutions

Since 1978, the Chinese government has been trying to slow down desertification by planting a huge line of trees, known as China's Great Green Wall. These trees were intended to stop the Gobi Desert from expanding. However, most of the trees have died as there isn't enough water in the soil to support them. The surviving trees have only managed to stop desertification in some areas.

Only **15%** of the
66 billion trees
planted in China's Great
Green Wall have survived.

Extreme weather

Scientists believe that climate change is making extreme weather, such as hurricanes, heat waves and heavy rain, more common and more extreme. These events can have a devastating impact.

Hurricanes

Hurricanes, also known as tropical cyclones or typhoons, are the strongest tropical storms. They are powered by warm, wet air that sits near the surface of the ocean.

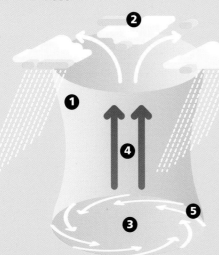

❶ Warm, wet air rises from the surface of the ocean.

❷ This air **condenses** higher up to form clouds.

❸ An area of low pressure forms near the surface of the water.

❹ The low-pressure area sucks in more warm air, which rises up and is pushed out at the top.

❺ Air quickly flows around the low-pressure area in a spiral.

This process happens more quickly and more frequently when the air and water is warmer, which is happening as a result of global warming.

Each degree we warm the planet causes a 7 percent increase in moisture.

Rainfall

Warm air can hold more water than cool air. This means that warm clouds carry more water and drop more rain. As a result, the higher temperatures caused by global warming will result in more rainfall.

flooding

Almond trees in California can usually survive periods of flooding and drought.

drought

Drought

Warm air makes water **evaporate** more quickly. This can cause soil to dry out, resulting in periods of drought. Some areas, such as California, are already experiencing alternating periods of droughts and flooding because of climate change.

Heat waves

As the Earth gets warmer, periods of extreme heat are becoming more common. In early 2018, southern Australia experienced a heat wave so severe that the roads melted in some places. Heat waves also increase the risk of dangerous forest fires. People who live near the already warm equator are at risk of deadly humid heat waves, in which the body can't cool down because the air is too wet for sweat to evaporate.

Cold weather

Some scientists are concerned that rising temperatures in the Arctic are destroying the polar vortex—a circle of strong winds that keeps cold air trapped in the Arctic. If the polar vortex were destroyed, the cold Arctic air would be free to travel across the northern hemisphere, causing freezing temperatures and heavy snow.

One-third of the world faces deadly heat waves because of climate change.

Hurricane Harvey

In August 2017, Hurricane Harvey hit the Caribbean and the south coast of the United States. It was the wettest storm in U.S. history, probably as a result of climate change. The heavy rains caused serious damage across the U.S. state of Texas.

FACT FILE

LOCATION:
The Caribbean and southern United States

MAXIMUM RECORDED RAINFALL:
60 inches (152 cm)

HIGHEST FLOOD LEVEL:
9.8 feet (3 m)

On the move

Hurricane Harvey formed in the eastern Caribbean. It then traveled northwest, hitting a few Caribbean islands and crossing the southeast coast of Mexico. The hurricane paused over the state of Texas for a few days, dropping huge amounts of rain. It then moved northeast towards Louisiana before dying away.

Wind and rain

The hurricane brought extreme weather, from winds of 130 miles per hour (210 kph) to extremely heavy rain. Scientists believe that climate change increased the rainfall of Hurricane Harvey by nearly 20 percent, as warmer air can hold more water.

Flooding

Hurricane Harvey resulted in serious floods. This was partly due to the heavy rain, but also to a storm surge—a side effect of the storm that made sea levels rise along the coast. Reservoirs built to trap rainwater burst their banks and flooded, which made the problem even worse.

People used boats to get around in the flooded streets of Houston, Texas, after Hurricane Harvey.

The weight of the water in Houston made the city temporarily sink by 0.8 inches (2 cm).

Houston

The city of Houston, Texas, was particularly affected by Hurricane Harvey. It is a low-lying city which was quickly flooded by the storm surge. It is also built on clay soil, and water does not drain through it easily. Many other low-lying coastal cities around the world will be similarly affected by storms in the future.

Evacuation

A state of emergency was called as Hurricane Harvey moved closer to the southern states. Around 30,000 people evacuated their homes and moved to higher ground to escape the storm. However, not everyone was able to get away. Emergency services carried out over 13,000 rescues, and 107 people were killed.

Recovery

The damage caused by Hurricane Harvey in the U.S. will cost more than $125 billion to repair. Hundreds of thousands of homes were flooded or damaged by high winds. Many roads, businesses, and public services, such as schools, were also affected.

High winds and heavy rain did much damage to this house in Texas.

Stopping climate change

Solving the problem of climate change involves stopping temperatures from rising further and gradually bringing them back down to a natural level. Everyone has a part to play in this process, from governments and businesses to individual people.

Fighting back

The most important step in fighting climate change is to stop more damage from being done. To do so, we need to reduce the amount of greenhouse gases in the atmosphere. We can do this by burning fewer fossil fuels and reducing cattle farming. We can also plant more trees and prevent deforestation, so that there are more plants to absorb extra carbon dioxide from the atmosphere.

Climate change agreements

Many countries around the world have signed climate change agreements that promise they will reduce the amount of greenhouse gases they release. In theory, this should help to control climate change around the world. However, as countries set their own targets and receive no penalties if they don't meet them, these agreements may not help much.

One small step

Solving climate change can seem scary and overwhelming. However, there are things that we can all do to help. Walk or cycle rather than take the car. Write a letter to a politician and find out what is being done to reduce the use of fossil fuels. These small steps can help to protect the planet.

Climate change deniers

Some people have doubts about climate change. Some believe that the climate is changing naturally, while others think that it isn't changing at all. However, since nearly all climate scientists state that evidence suggests that humans are responsible for climate change, it's interesting to think about why people might deny climate change is happening. Some people deny climate change because they don't want to alter the way they live to fix it. Others don't understand it or think it is a hoax.

Catching carbon

Scientists are also experimenting with new techniques to control climate change. One is to turn carbon dioxide into a liquid and inject it deep into Earth in empty oil or water reserves. The carbon dioxide would then be trapped underground. However, this has not been tested long term and there is a risk it might escape, damage the surrounding rock, or have other negative effects.

Taking the train rather than flying is one way of producing fewer greenhouse gases.

Glossary

condense To change from a gas to a liquid

conflict Fighting between different groups

conservationist Someone whose job it is to protect nature

decompose To break down

deforestation Cutting down trees and clearing the land

dilute To make a liquid weaker by adding another liquid to it

drought A period when there isn't enough water

ecosystem All the living things in an area

erosion The breaking down of rocks and movement of sand and soil

evaporate To change from a liquid to a gas

fossil fuel A fuel that comes from the ground, such as coal, oil, or gas

graze To eat grass

greenhouse gas A gas that traps heat in the atmosphere, such as carbon dioxide

Industrial Revolution A period in the 1700s and 1800s in which products started to be made in factories, rather than by hand in homes

livestock Animals that are raised for their meat or other products

photosynthesis The process by which plants use energy from the Sun to create their own food

pollinate To transfer pollen from one plant to another, producing seeds

refugee Someone who has been forced to leave their home

renewable Describes something that can be reproduced and will not run out

Learning More

Books

Bow, James. **Earth's Climate Change: Carbon Dioxide Overload.** Crabtree Publishing, 2016.

Dickmann, Nancy. **Using Renewable Energy.** Crabtree Publishing, 2019.

Steele, Philip. **Analyzing Climate Change: Asking Questions, Evaluating Evidence, and Designing Solutions.** Cavendish Square, 2018.

Websites

climatekids.nasa.gov/climate-change-meaning/
Get the facts about climate change.

www.earthday.org/climate-change-quiz/
Take a quiz about climate change.

www.bbc.co.uk/gardening/gardening_with_children/homegrownprojects_compost. shtml Learn how to make a compost bin.

Index